Dedicated to
Those who cared and shared.

German-American Cookbook

Edited by William D. Setzekorn

ISBN: 0-7596-6876-0

This book is printed on acid free paper.

Printed in the United States of America

1stBooks – rev. 01/10/02

CONTENTS

INTRODUCTION

In the Fall of 1848, a failed social revolution in Germany sent thousands of self-imposed political exiles and their families swarming across German borders, many finding their way to America. Although Germans had migrated to the United States prior to 1848, no group made such an impact on the American scene than the 58,000 German emigrants of 1848 known as the "Forty-Eighters". Many, as my own immigrant ancestors did, arrived through the Port of New Orleans and traveled by paddlewheeler to settle the rich Mississippi Valley, concentrating their settlement in the area of Southern Illinois from Chester in the south to as far north as the new railhead at Quincy. As naïve as it now may seem, they brought with them an ideal of founding a perfect Teutonic society, a "New Germany", in America.

The 1848 migration caused an intellectual and military drain in Germany. Many of their citizens of greatest vitality left to find in the United States a new arena for their lifework. Forty-Eighters enlisted in the Northern Army during the Civil War proportionally far in excess of any immigrant group. German immigrants held more than half of all Major-Generalships allotted to non-citizens and provided nine brigadier-Generals. One historian claims that one in every three German-born males of military age in the United States at the time of the Civil War offered his life for his adopted country, a remarkable record and far in excess of any other immigrant group. Even with full participation in American politics and culture, their dream of a free Teutonic state in America did not completely die out until 1917 when World War I made anything short of complete and unequivocal allegiance to their adopted land quite impossible. German-language schools, churches, newspapers and gymnasia disappeared overnight. German cuisine, however, did not.

This is intended to be a light-hearted dip into representative dishes to sample the state of the art of German-American cooking in the Mississippi Valley today. No attempt has been made to separate plain fare from the dishes one might fix for company. It is an anthology of recipes stemming from family, restaurant and peasant kitchens of Europe, but it is not a translation of a German cookbook. European cooking is different. Their recipes usually presume a large amount of cooking knowledge of the cook, require special skills and complicated ingredients. Recipes in this book are easy. They are intended for the home cook and the home kitchen calling for ingredients available in American markets today using only appliances and utensils found in an average American kitchen. All are tried and true. Most of these recipes were brought to Illinois by our ancestors in 1848 and have undergone six generations of loving adaption. For those of German descent who did not inherit them, perhaps this book will replace that which was lost and hopefully even restore some fine old family culinary traditions.

This book is the merger of two of my lifetime interests - my family roots and German cuisine. Those who know me best may be amused by my editorship of a cookbook. I have been told, "I thought the only culinary utensil in your house was a can opener". Although I definitely am not a serious chef, I am a serious eater, an art which I have been practicing for over 65 years, and I suggest that alone gives me the right. I first became interested in German food when I lived briefly as an exchange student with a family in Münster, Westfalen. The head of this family, Ernst Frei, had been an army cook. This was shortly after the war when meat was scarce and very expensive. Herr Frei proved so masterful a cook that he was able to serve a different meatless potato dish as our entrée each night for a week without receiving a single complaint. Some of his recipes from my collection found their way into this book.

I have generally found chefs quite willing to oblige when I sent pad and pencil back to the kitchen with a request for the recipe of some dish that I had just enjoyed. Chefs of German restaurants from the Hofbrauhaus in Munich, Luchow's in New York City, to der Alpen Haus in Los Altos, California are just some that have generously contributed. These have been suitably and professionally edited for suitability for use of the American household chef.

I wish to acknowledge the generosity of the many cousins and friends without whose contributions of family recipes this work would not have been possible and ethnic groups such as the German Club of Hermann, Missouri, a town settled by Germans in mid-nineteenth century of the same stock and background as my own, who collected German recipes that had been preserved in their families and printed a Hermann-German Cookbook from which they have graciously allowed me to steal a few which I believe Anna Dorothea Setzekorn herself might well have prepared in 1848. I am grateful to my translator, Ann Sherwin, for all her work.

I am in debt to my son, Jeff, and his wife, Jeannette. Jeff helped pay his way through college as a chef in Northern California supper clubs and at the East Bay Holiday Inn. Jeannette is a journeyman chef in her own right. They proofread and gave generous input into this project.

Best wishes and PROSIT!

WDS
6 January 2000
Somerset, CA

APPETIZERS

HUHNLEBERPASTETE
(Chicken Liver Pâté)

This tasty French filling for pastry has been adopted by German-Americans as a rich spread for crackers. In Germany it is used in the French manner.

1/2 pound onions, sliced
1/2 cup poultry fat
1/2 cup chicken stock or bouillon
1 pound fresh pork liver
2 pounds chicken livers
3/4 pound salt pork cut in thin strips
1 teaspoon salt
1/2 teaspoon pepper
3 cloves
1/8 teaspoon thyme
1 bay leaf, crumpled
3 eggs, beaten
1 cup heavy cream
1 cup cooking sherry
2 tablespoons cornstarch
2 tablespoons butter

Cook onions in goose or chicken fat and stock until they are transparent and tender. Wash liver and lard it with strips of salt pork, then cut into small pieces and place in a saucepan with onions, the fat they cooked in, salt, pepper, cloves, thyme, and the bay leaf. Cover with cold water and simmer in covered pan for about two hours, or until the liver is quite tender. Drain, finely grind liver and onions and mix with eggs, cream and most of the sherry.

Moisten cornstarch smoothly with the remainder of the sherry and beat into the liver mixture until it forms a smooth paste. Pack into a crock or mold and pour melted butter over the top. Keep covered in the refrigertor. Cut into slices, serves 10.

HINT: Other recipes call for 2 or 3 chopped anchovies or finely minced truffles for variation in flavor. The contributor recommends a Josephshofer Auslese, a select dry Moselle to complement the rich pâté.

TASCHENKREBSKANAPEES
(Crabmeat Canapes)

1 package (8 oz.) cream cheese
6½ ounces canned crab meat
2 tablespoons mayonnaise
2 tablespoons Parmesan cheese
1/2 cup cheddar cheese, grated
2 green onions, chopped
1 teaspoon Worcestershire sauce
paprika
1 package dinner rolls

Mix ingredients together. Separate each roll into three, making a total of 36 canapes. Fill with spread and flute edges. Cook at 350°F. for 15 minutes or until nicely brown.

GEFÜLLTE PILZE
(Stuffed Mushrooms)

12 large (about 1/2 pound)
fresh mushrooms
1 small onion
1/4 cup Parmesan cheese, grated
salt
pepper
1 tablespoon margarine or salad oil

Remove mushroom stems and set caps aside. Chop onion and stems. Sautè onion in skillet with salad oil over medium heat, add mushroom stems, salt and pepper to taste. Continue to sautè for about fifteen minutes until stems are dry. Stuff the mushroom caps with sautèd mixture and top with Parmesan cheese. Arrange stuffed mushroom caps on a greased cookie sheet and broil in oven for 3 to 4 minutes.

PARTY DIPS

The following party dips are German-American contributions using ingredients suggested by European recipes. If they eat dip in Germany at all, I am sure it is a recent phenomenon and if they have adopted this German-American custom, perhaps they have also accepted the English word, "Dip" but it looks rather strange attached to a German word.

TASCHENKREBSDIP
(Crab Dip)

1 package (8 oz.) cream cheese
6½ ounces canned crab meat
2 tablespoon onion, finely chopped
2 tablespoon milk
1/2 teaspoon creamed horseradish
1/4 teaspoon salt
pepper
1/3 cup sliced and toasted almonds

Combine softened cream cheese with other ingredients except almonds. Bake in baking dish at 350°F. for 15 minutes or until nicely brown. Scatter almonds on top. Serve in chafing dish for dipping with toast points or wafers.

MUSCHELDIP
(Clam and Cheese Dip)

5 ounces cheddar cheese
2 cans minced clams
5 green onions

Mix ingredients together and bake until mixture bubbles. Pour into chafing dish for dipping and serve with toast points or crackers.

SOUPS

BOHNENSUPPE MIT SCHWEINEHAXEN
(Bean Soup with Ham Hocks)

Nothing new here. What we call "cornbread and beans" or "navy bean soup" is a favorite everywhere. I am including it knowing that you don't need this book to tell you how to cook bean soup.

1 pkg. dried beans, small
northern or similar
3 medium-sized ham hocks
1 stalk celery, chopped
1 onion, chopped
salt
pepper
garlic, clove or powdered

Place beans in soup kettle, cover with water and soak overnight. Wash beans thoroughly by pouring them in colander and rinsing them thoroughly before returning to kettle. Add ham hocks, onion, and celery. Season to taste with salt, pepper and garlic. Fill kettle with water to just cover the ham hocks. Bring to boil, cover and simmer for about one hour or until beans are soft. Check from time to time for doneness and add water as necessary while cooking.

Serve with warm cornbread (box mix will do) and butter.

MUSCHELSUPPE
(Mussel or Clam Soup)

Here again, little neck clams may be substituted for mussels if not readily available or out of season.

36 mussels
1/2 cup olive oil
1 clove garlic
2 tablespoons tomato sauce
1/2 teaspoon salt
1 tiny red pepper (optional)
1/2 teaspoon oregano

Wash mussels well. Place oil in deep pan, add garlic and brown. Add tomato sauce, pepper, salt and mussels. Cook over high flame until all mussels are open. Add oregano and cook about a minute longer. Serve the mussels and sauce in soup bowls or plates poured over french or garlic bread.

KARTOFFELSUPPE
(Potato Soup)

1 pound potatoes
1 or 2 tomatoes
1 yellow turnip
1 stalk celery
1 medium onion
2 tablespoons butter
1 tablespoon flour
1-1/2 quarts water
1 tablespoon salt
1 to 2 tablespoons sour cream
parsley

Dice potatoes and vegetables. Melt butter and heat vegetables in it without browning them. Sprinkle with flour. Add water (or beef stock) and salt. Cook 25 to 35 minutes until done. When vegetables are soft, enrich with sour cream and garnish with parsley. Sprinkle with croutons. Serves 4-6.

SPARGELSUPPE
(Asparagus Soup)

1 pound asparagus
1 quart water, slightly salted
4 tablespoons flour
4 tablespoons butter
1 egg yolk
2 tablespoons cream

Clean the asparagus and cut into inch-long pieces. Cook until tender in slightly salted water. Make a white sauce by stirring flour into melted butter, adding dashes of hot asparagus water to fully dissolve the flour. Add to soup stock and thicken with beaten egg yolk and cream.

Serves 4.

KÖNIGINSUPPE
(Royal Chicken Soup)

"Soup fit for a queen" or literally, "Queen's Soup". This chicken soup recipe has come down to us in several variations. I do not know about availability of chicken fat so you are on your own.

3 tablespoons chicken fat (real or artificial)
3 tablespoons onion, minced
1/4 cup flour
4 cups chicken broth
1/2 cup chicken meat, shredded

Heat chicken fat and cook the onion in it for about ten minutes. Add flour and stir constantly, gradually adding broth until mixture reaches the boiling point. Add chicken meat and cook over low heat another ten minutes. Garnish with sauteed mushrooms or minced parsley.

Serves 4.

SEAFOOD

FISCH MIT DILL
German-American "Dilly Fisch" or
Fish fillets in a creamy dill sauce.

Even though this traditional old German recipe has been up-dated somewhat (aluminum foil?) I still can imagine our immigrant grandmothers using it to prepare pan fish from the Werra River or catfish from the Kaskaskia caught by our forefathers on cane poles. I tested it with turbot, but any firm-fleshed fish should do as well.

1 pound fish fillets
3 tablespoons butter
1 teaspoon salt
1 bay leaf
1 medium onion, finely sliced
1/4 cup dry white wine
2 beaten egg yolks
1/2 cup sour cream
2 tablespoons fresh dill, chopped
or 1-1/2 teaspoons dried dill weed

Line a roasting pan with aluminum foil. Place a double layer of fish fillets over the buttered foil. Sprinkle each layer with salt and several dollops of butter. Add a bay leaf and the sliced onion. Pour the wine over and fold the aluminum foil over the top forming a tightly-sealed packet. Bake at 375°F. for about 20 minutes, turning the packetover after ten minutes. (The original recipe called for a total cooking time of only ten minutes, but 12 in a test run in my oven this proved to be not long enough so, for best results, check from time to time and when the fish flakes easily when tested with a fork, you will know it is done.)

Remove the fillets to a hot platter, cover with the onion and set aside. Pour about two tablespoons of the hot pan juices into the egg yolks and beat. Gradually stir in and beat the rest of the pan juices, sour cream and dill. This sauce can be either served on the side or, as I prefer, poured over the fillets and served as a casserole garnished with lemon wedges. Serve the rest of the white wine at the table. *Zeller Schwartze Katz,* a fine dry white Moselle wine goes well with this dish, as it does with all seafood and is my favorite.

MUSCHEL von der SEE
(Mussels Marinière)

Our immigrant family supplemented their diet with freshwater mussels found in local streams and rivers in Southern Illinois. These bivalve mollusks come in 1000 known species and are common to streams, lakes and ponds throughout the world. Mussels have received a bad name in this country due to paralytic shellfish poisoning, commonly known as mussel poisoning, identified with some subspecies of mussels. Just like mushrooms, if you are not an expert on this subject, leave mussel gathering to those who are and follow local public health quarantine regulations, as this problem is seasonal and do not rely on the various folk tales as to methods for differentiating between poisonous and edible varieties. It is best to ask your grocer to obtain them for you. They are raised commercially these days for poultry and livestock feed. If this has not scared you off, you will find this land-locked seafood a tasty treat. If not, substitute imported soft-shelled clams. The result with be a different tasting dish but equally tasty.

24 mussels
2 chopped shallots (scallions or
onions may be substituted)
1/4 teaspoon pepper
1 pinch of thyme
1 cup dry white wine
2 tablespoons chopped parsley
1 tablespoon flour
1 tablespoon butter

Wash mussels and place in deep kettle. Add shallots, pepper, thyme, wine and parsley. Do not salt. Cover, bring to boil and simmer for six to eight minutes or until the shells open, stirring once or twice.

Remove mussels to deep serving dish or individual soup bowls and keep warm. Combine flour and butter.

Bring to a boil and stir in flour and butter. Cook, stirring constantly until it thickens. Pour over the mussels and sprinkle with parsley. This recipe serves 2 as an entrée.Some recipes call for a dash of cayenne pepper and a clove of garlic. A famous French restaurant lets the mussels marinate in the sauce for three days before re-heating and serving.

Hint - Since it is easier to cook the mussels first and let them open naturally rather than opening them by hand before cooking, there may be some sand left in the bottom of the kettle. If so, strain the kettle juice through cheesecloth into a sauce pan.

HUMMER THERMIDOR
(Lobster Thermidor)

O.K., so our immigrant ancestors had no source of lobster in Southern Illinois and probably did not have this recipe anyway, but my research revealed Lobster Thermidor to be a favorite at the best German restaurants, and since I am having so much fun testing these recipes and it is going so well, I decided to test and share this one. Where I come from, Lobsters come in two ways, pre-cooked and live. I chose the former.

2 two-pound cooked lobsters, frozen
4 tablespoons butter
1 small onion or shallot, diced
6 mushroom caps, diced
1/2 teaspoon salt
1/2 teaspoon paprika
1 cup sherry
1/2 cup heavy cream
1/4 teaspoon mustard
1/2 teaspoon Worcestershire sauce

Thaw lobsters in the refrigerator for twenty-four hours or at room temperature for twelve hours before cooking. Do not place in warm water to thaw. They must be fully defrosted before cooking.

Boil water and plunge the lobsters into the water for two to three minutes. (Yes I know they are already pre-cooked, but trust me on this one).

Remove from water and cut lobsters open on the underside lengthwise through shell and tail with shears and crack claws. Remove all meat from shells and claws. Clean the shells of other material found inside. There will be tomalley (green color) which is the critter's liver. This is edible and used in some recipes but not this one. Also you will find roe (red color and sometimes partially black and harmless). Drain excess water from the shells after cleaning by poking a hole in the lobster's mouth and holding it upside down for a few seconds. Set the shells aside and save for refilling.

Cut meat into small pieces and sauté in butter with onion or shallot and mushrooms. Season with salt and paprika. After about six minutes add sherry, cream, mustard and Worchestershire sauce. Simmer until thickened and reduced. The mixture should be very thick. Fill the shells.

Lobster is usually served with mayonnaise on the side and a salad garnished with mayonnaise or olive-oil. If sherry is well selected, i.e. sipping sherry rather than cooking sherry, serve rest at table. Or, better yet, since cheap sherry is fine for cooking but can be nasty for drinking, save the remaining sherry for another time and serve the lobsters with a full-bodied Neufchâtel or Moselle. Serves 2.

HINT: I made this test with one small 1# lobster without reducing the recipe. The little lobster was excellent but I had a great deal of filling left over. This was frozen and served as stock for a delicious Bouillabaisse (fish stew) another day.

FLUSSKREBS
(Freshwater Crawfish)

I was amazed to find these rascals at my local store, just like I used to catch in the streams in Southern Illinois with my maternal Scot-Irish grandfather. I had forgotten how good they are.

30 large crawfish
1 tablespoon butter
salt
2 cups sour cream
1 heaping tablespoon bread crumbs
1 heaping tablespoon chopped fresh dill

21

Scrub the crawfish thoroughly and plunge them into unsalted boiling water for a minute or two. Drain and rinse. Place crawfish in saucepan with melted butter and simmer for ten minutes or until the crawfish turn red. Salt lightly, add sour cream, bread crumbs and dill. Simmer, tightly covered, for another fifteen minutes. Serve at once. Serves 5 or 6.

Caution: overcooking spoils the taste.

FRIKASEE VON FROSCHKEULEN
(Frogleg Fricassee)

I remember hearing stories of my father and his friends going "frog gigging" at night with lantern and a spear-like "gig" in the Kaskaskia River bottoms of Southern Illinois and was pleased to find that the dwellers along the Werra River do the same thing but fricassee them instead of merely frying them as most Americans do.

12 whole frogs, cleaned
2 tablespoons olive oil
1 small onion, chopped
1 cove garlic, chopped
1/4 cup white wine
1/2 teaspoon salt
1/2 teaspoon pepper
1/4 cup dried mushrooms, soaked in
water for 1/2 hour
2 tablespoons flour
1 tablespoon parsley, chopped
2 egg yolks, lightly beaten
1 tablespoon lemon juice
12 thin slices French bread,
toasted

Skin frogs and remove legs. Place legs in cold water and allow to stand two hours. Brown onion and garlic in oil and add wine. When wine has evaporated, add frog bodies, dried mushrooms, salt and pepper. Add just enough water to cover and simmer for one hour in covered pan. Strain this broth and retain.

Flour the frog legs and add them to the broth. Cook slowly about thirty minutes, stirring occasionally. When legs are tender, add chopped parsley. Remove pan from heat and add two egg yolks and lemon juice. Mix well and serve on toast. Serves 4.

POULTRY
and
GAME BIRDS

REBHUHN MIT ORANGENKRAUT
(Pheasant with Orange Sauerkraut)

This is a combination of two German recipes. The oranges in the sauerkraut are not in the original recipe but I found kraut done this way in a small delightful inn in the medieval German town of Eisenach, not far from our homeland in Thüringen and thought it a wonderful variation on ordinary sauerkraut.

1 Pheasant (partridge, grouse or
other gamebird)
1/2 lemon
Juniper berries
Bacon or salt pork slices
Brandy
Heavy cream
Oranges
Butter
Sauerkraut
Salt
Pepper

Singe, clean and draw the birds. Wash thoroughly and dry. Rub cavity and skin with lemon. Place two juniper berries into the cavity of each bird. Wrap pork or bacon slices around the birds and truss them. Roast in hot (400°F.) oven twenty minutes, basting frequently. Five minutes before the birds are done, increase oven heat to 450°F. and remove bacon slices. Brown breasts thoroughly. Blaze brandy by lighting it in a warmed ladle and pour over birds. Remove birds to a platter and keep warm. Stir cream into pan bastings and simmer over moderate heat three or four minutes. Pour over birds.

For each quart of sauerkraut, use one orange. Peel oranges, removing all white skin and cut into pieces. Sauté in hot butter using 1/4 cup of butter for each quart of sauerkraut and orange slices for three to four minutes. Drain sauerkraut and add to orange. Season with salt and pepper to taste. Cover, simmer for ten minutes and drain.

Serve each bird on a mound of stiff rich mashed potatoes. Surround with sauerkraut. Platter may be further decorated with thin orange slices and parsley or water-cress sprigs.

The traditional way Germans serve pheasants is to reassemble the bird after it has been carved and decorate it with its own colorful feathers to simulate a live pheasant. I have seen this done in a German restaurant and it made a dramatic presentation. I doubt if our ancestors bothered with it, but it might be fun to try on an especially festive occasion.

CHICKEN MONTCLAIRE
(a.k.a. "Yummy Chicken")

This recipe is not German at all but one of my five-star favorites and I include it with the admonition that if you don't try anything else in this cookbook, try this one!

2-3# chicken cut up
1 pkg. Lipton dry onion soup mix
1 bottle creamy French dressing
1 can (16 oz.) cranberry sauce

Mix all ingredients (except chicken) together and place in refrigerator until time to start. Cut up, wash and dry the chicken. Salt and pepper it and place in a baking dish. Pour the sauce over the chicken and bake uncovered for one hour and fifteen minutes in 350° oven. Enjoy!

ENTCHEN MIT ROTKOHL
(Duckling Braised in Red Cabbage)

3-4# duck or other game bird
Salt
Pepper
1 medium-sized head of red cabbage,
shredded
Juice of 1/2 lemon
1/2 cup diced salt pork
1 medium-sized chopped onion
2 tablespoons flour
1 cup red wine (a hearty Rhine wine)
1 or 2 teaspoons sugar
1 teaspoon caraway seeds

Rub duckling cavity with salt and pepper. Truss the bird and prick skin all over with tines of a fork Place in shallow roasting pan and roast in hot (425°F.) oven ten minutes. Lower oven temperature to moderate (350°F.) and roast fifty minutes longer. Remove duckling from pan and keep warm.

While duck is roasting, rinse cabbage with boiling water and drain immediately. Sprinkle with lemonjuice to perserve color. Cook salt pork in heavy kettle over medium heat until transparent, add onion and flour and cook five minutes stirring constantly. Add cabbage, red wine, sugar, pepper and carraway seeds. Cover and simmer over low heat for about thirty minutes or until duck is roasted. Transfer duck into the kettle with the cabbage. Cover and simmer for forty-five minutes to an hour or until bird is quite tender. Place duckling on a hot platter and serve the red cabbage in a separate dish. Serve the rest of the red wine at the table. It and a potato dish make good accompaniments.

HÜHNCHEN MIT SCHWÄMMEN
(Chicken in Mushroom Sauce)

8 chicken beasts
1 lemon
salt
pepper
garlic powder
butter
1 can cream of mushroom soup
1 pt. mushrooms, chopped
1/2 cup dry sherry

Rub chicken breasts with lemon, salt, pepper and garlic powder. Butter a flat baking dish and pour in contents of cream of mushroom soup and fresh chopped mushrooms.

Cover tightly with foil and place in 325°F. oven for about 35 minutes or until done. Remove foil and brown slightly under broiler. Just before serving, add sherry, replace foil cover and cook for about five minutes in a hot (450°F.) oven.

Serves 8.

HÜHNCHEN IN WEINSOSSE
(Chicken in Wine Sauce)

6 chicken breasts
1 teaspoons butter
1 teaspoon cooking oil
3 tablespoons cornstarch
1½ cup chicken broth or bouillon
1/3 cup milk
1/3 cup lemon juice
1/3 cup dry white wine
3 cloves garlic, crushed
1/4 cup Parmesan cheese, grated

Prepare chicken breasts and set aside. Brown chicken on both sides in butter over medium heat. Place chicken in large baking dish which has been sprayed with non-stick spray.

Pour cooking oil into hot skillet Stir in cornstarch and small amount of chicken broth. Stir until smooth. Remove pan from heat and slowly add 1 cup of broth return to heat and add remaining broth, milk lemon juice, wine and garlic, stirring constantly. When sauce has thickened slightly, pour over chicken breasts. Sprinkle with Parmesan and bake in hot (350°F.) oven for about thirty minutes. Serve over rice, or with a potato dish and the rest of the dry white wine such as a dry Moselle. Serves 6.

HUHN IM TOPF
("Chicken in a pot", a favorite German casserole dish)

3-4 pound stewing chicken
1 small carrot (optional)
1 small onion (optional)
1 or 2 whole peppers
4 tablespoons butter
6 tablespoons flour
3 cups cream
1 pint fresh mushrooms (or two
small cans)
1/2 cup green peppers, chopped
2 medium onions
1 tablespoon butter
1/4 cup pimento, sliced
1 cup bread crumbs, buttered

Place hen in pan and add cold water just to cover. Add salt, carrot, onion, and a whole pepper. Cover tightly, heat to boiling and simmer gently until chicken is very tender (2 to 3 hours). Cool in liquid. Pull meat from bones leaving it in rather large pieces. Melt butter in skillet, add flour, cream, and blend with one cup of the chicken stock which has been strained, stirring constantly and slowly until thick and smooth. Sauté onions, green pepper, and fresh mushrooms in butter. Add these and pimento to sauce and season to taste. Place alternate layers of chicken and sauce in a large greased casserole covered with buttered bread crumbs. Bake at 350°F. for 35 to 40 minutes. Serves 4.

MASTGANS MIT FRUCHT
(Roast Goose with Fruit Stuffing)

The custom of serving roast goose for Christmas was brought here by the Germans and is still the traditional festive fowl for most of Europe. Fresh ones are sometimes available only if you order well ahead, but frozen goose is usually readily available.

1 young goose (about 9 pounds)
1 package mixed dried fruits (11 oz.)
1 cup orange juice
10 slices white bread, toasted and diced
1/2 teaspoon ground ginger
1/2 teaspoon ground cinnamon
1/2 teaspoon ground nutmeg
1/4 teaspoon ground cloves
apricot brandy

Thaw frozen goose 2 or 3 days in refrigerator. Remove giblets and any excess fat from inside goose. Rinse with cold water and drain. Dice fruit and combine with orange juice in small bowl; let stand about 30 minutes. Combine bread and spice in large bowl, pour fruit mixture over and toss until moistened. (Mixture will seem somewhat dry). Stuff about one cup of fruit dressing in neck cavity; fold skin over and hold in place with wing tip or skewers. Stuff remaining dressing into body cavity and close vent with skewers.

Place goose on oven rack in shallow pan, prick with meat fork in fatty areas around wings and legs. Do not cover. Do not add water. Roast in slow (325°F.) oven for three hours. Remove accumulated fat from pan once each hour. Brush with apricot brandy and roast for an additional thirty minutes, brushing with brandy several more times. Remove to heated platter, carve breast into thin slices and separate drumsticks and thighs at point.

Place the roasting pan with drippings on top of the range. Make gravy by stirring flour into fat, add two cups water and boil two or three minutes until smooth and thickened. Serve with goose. Accompany with red cabbage, mashed potatoes, nd cherry strudel for dessert. A full-bodied white Rhone wine goes well with goose. Serves 6.

HINT: There is little waste on a goose. In Germany, rendered goose-fat sandwiches are a delicacy as well as the cracklings, gizzards and liver, eaten separately if not made into giblet gravy.

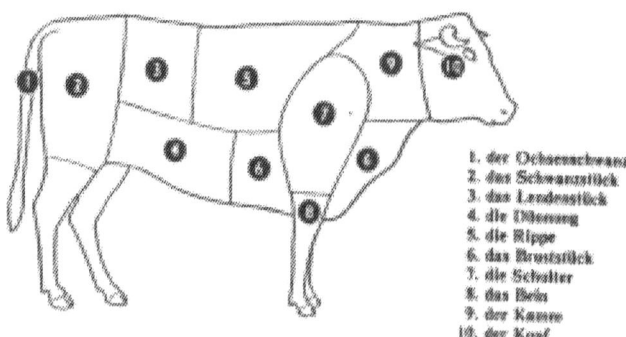

1. der Ochsenschwanz
2. das Schwanzstück
3. das Lendenstück
4. die Dünnung
5. die Rippe
6. das Bruststück
7. die Schulter
8. das Bein
9. der Kamm
10. der Kopf

MEAT and BIG GAME

KALBSBRATEN
(German Veal Roast)

This is roasting in the German way - atop the stove. It allows you to fix small roasts without them shrinking to nothing as they tend to do when oven-roasted. This recipe can be used with beef roasts as well as veal. I tested with a London Broil and it turned out scrumptious.

2# veal roast, trimmed and tied
if necessary.
Salt
Pepper
1 tablespoon flour
2 tablespoons butter
1/2 cup dry white wine
1 medium-sized onion
1 pinch of thyme
1/2 cup sour cream

Rub veal with salt and pepper and dust with flour. Brown both sides well in butter in heavy frying pan or casserole dish. Add about 1-1/2" of wine. Add onion and thyme. Cover tightly and simmer for about one hour, or until done. This will vary with cut of roast and thickness so check for doneness from time to time.

Remove from heat and stir in sour cream. Return to heat but do not allow to boil. Slice meat and arrange on a heated platter. Pour sauce over meat and garnish with parsley. Serve with a plain potato dish and tossed salad. Serve the rest of the wine at the table. As you probably know by now, my favorite dry white wine is *Schwartze Katz*, a Moselle wine from Zell and it works perfectly here. Serves 3 or 4.

SCHWEINEHAXEN mit SAUERKRAUT
(Ham Hocks and Sauerkraut)

This is a very common way of fixing sauerkraut. We find it throughout Germany and in the German-American communities as well.

6 medium-sized ham hocks
2 pounds sauerkraut
2 large bay leaves
6 sprigs parsley
6 sprigs green celery tops
2 tablespoons caraway seeds

Wash the hocks thoroughly and place them in a kettle, cover with water, and simmer for one hour. Remove hocks and set them aside. Add the sauerkraut to the kettle water and add bay leaves, parsley, and celery all tied together. Place the ham hocks back into the kettle, cover and boil for about another two hours or until both meat and sauerkraut are tender. Caraway seeds (optional) may be added about thirty minutes before the end of the cooking time. Drain and place the sauerkraut on a platter. Serve with plain boiled potatoes or purée of dried peas. (see *Erbsenpüree* under "Casseroles and Vegetables").

This is usually served with lots of beer.

WIENER SCHNITZEL - Basic
(Breaded Veal Cutlet)

This is probably the most common of all German entrées. Schnitzel to Germans is what the hamburger is to Americans. As soon as I land in Frankfort, I search out my favorite country inn in Kronberg and have Schnitzel and a pilsner. Only then does it seem I am back in our home land. This recipe is simple. When done correctly, they simply sizzle!

1 3/4 pound veal cutlet, 1/2" thick
salt
pepper
1 egg
1/8 cup milk
1/4 cup bread crumbs
cooking oil
1/4 cup flour
1 lemon
parsley

Pound cutlet with tenderizing hammer (butchers do this if asked) and rub with seasoning. Beat egg with a little milk then dip cutlet in egg, flour, and bread crumbs. Brown in a minimum amount of cooking oil over high heat for ten to fifteen minutes each side. As soon as they are golden brown, reduce heat and continue frying until they are done clear through. Serve dry and crisp, garnished with lemon sections and parsley.

Schnitzels are usually served with a vegetable dish, a tossed salad and a dry white wine. *Piesporter Goldtröp-fchen Auslese* can't be beat, though I prefer beer. Serves 2.

TIP: pre-seasoned croutons, crushed, make great bread crumbs.

Since German-American contributors have given me a number of variations on this theme, I am including some other Schnitzels. Pork cutlets and pork tenderloin may be substituted for veal in all schnitzel recipes.

REHSCHNITZEL
(Venison Cutlet)

4 venison steaks or cutlets
salt
pepper
4 tablespoons butter
2 tomatoes, halved
1 medium onion, sliced
1 tablespoon flour
2 tablespoons red wine

Tenderize steaks well and season. Melt butter in a roasting pan or large casserole dish and brown steaks both sides at high heat. Add tomatoes, onion and wine. Reduce heat and simmer for about twenty minutes or until steaks are done through. Remove meat to a hot platter. To the pan fat add flour, salt, pepper and more wine. Strain and pour over meat. Serve with mashed potatoes or *Spätzle*. (See "Sauces and Miscellany" chapter for *Spätzle* recipe). A full-bodied red wine like Burgundy which will stand up to the flavor of game is best served with venison. Serves 4.

SCHNITZEL AU NATUREL
(Veal or other Cutlet)

This quick schnitzel recipe is so simple it's a natural.

1 3/4 pound cutlet, 1/2" thick
1 teaspoon olive oil
salt
pepper
2 tablespoons butter
paprika
1 lemon

Soak cutlet in milk for ten minutes. Dry, tenderize, and brush with oil and seasoning. Fry slowly in hot butter for about ten minutes, each side. When done, garnish with quartered lemon.

Serve with rice or dumplings, cauliflower, spinach or a tossed green salad. Serves 2.

RAHMSCHNITZEL
(Creamed veal cutlet)

1 3/4 pound veal cutlet, 1/2" thick
salt
pepper
2 tablespoons butter
paprika
1/4 teaspoon flour
2-3 tablespoons cream
1 lemon
parsley

Tenderize veal cutlet and season with salt and pepper. Fry on high heat about ten minutes each side or until done to suit. Remove cutlet to warm platter. Add flour and cream to pan fat, cook together until warm and pour over cutlet. Garnish with lemon slices, paprika and chopped parsley. Serve with dumplings, buttered rice, and/or a tossed salad. Serves 2.

SCHWEINEROSTBRATEN
(Roast Pork)

4 pork steaks, 3/4" thick
3 tablespoons catsup
2 tablespoons lemon juice
1/2 teaspoon mustard
1 teaspoon Worchestershire Sauce
2 tablespoons cooking oil.
1 large onion
1/4 cup

Combine catsup, lemon juice, mustard, and Worchestershire sauce, mix well and rub into each side of steaks. Brown slowly in small amount of cooking oil, about ten minutes each side. Arrange in a greased baking pan, top with onion slices, add water, cover and bake for one hour in 325° to 350°F. oven.

Serve with a plain potato dish, tossed salad and a dry white or rosé wine. Serves 4.

KÖNIGSBERGER KLOPSE
(Meat Balls Koenigsberg)

This is one of those traditional German dishes that has "traveled well". Don't let the long list of ingredients scare you, Klops are fun to make and a real gourmet treat.

1 slice French bread, 1" thick or
two hard rolls
1/2 pound ground beef
1/2 pound ground veal
1/2 pound ground pork (or liver)
2 eggs
1 tablespoon butter
1/4 cup finely minced onion
10 beef boullion cubes dissolved in
5 cups of water
3 tablespoons parsley, chopped
1-1/4 teaspoons salt
1/4 teaspoon paprika
1/2 teaspoon grated lemon rind
1 teaspoon lemon juice
1 teaspoon Worchestershire sauce

Have butcher grind meat twice to combine all three. (Actually, combination of beef and pork in equal amounts works almost as well).

Moisten bread or rolls with water; when soft, ring out and mix bread with meat. Sauté onion in butter until lightly browned, add to meat. Beat eggs well and add to meat mixture along with parsley, salt, paprika, lemon rind and juice, and Worchestershire sauce. Mix thoroughly and shape into 2 inch balls (will make about twelve).

Heat bouillon stock to boiling; drop balls in and simmer, covered, fifteen minutes. Remove Klops from stock with a slotted spoon and keep warm while preparing gravy.

Add four or five tablespoons of melted butter and four or five tablespoons of flour to stock. Cook until smooth and boiling. Season to taste with salt and paprika. Add two tablespoons of lemon juice, and two tablespoons of chopped parsley. Pour gravy over meatballs and reheat. Just before serving, sprinkle with bread crumbs. Serves 4.

Serve with boiled noodles or *Spaezle* (see "Sauces and Miscellany" chapter).

HINT: Contemporary German contributors suggest adding two tablespoons of capers and/or one or two boneless sardines to the gravy mixture. Also, some suggest using 1/3 to 1/2 cups crushed croutons for bread.

KLOPSE MIT PILZEN
(Meat Balls in Mushroom Sauce)

Purists can skip this one. This is a much simplified German-American alternative to the above recipe. Who says easy can't be good?

3/4 pound ground beef
1 egg, beaten
1 cup branflakes or crushed croutons
1/2 onion, finely diced
salt
pepper
1 dash cinnamon
1 dash nutmeg
1 can cream of mushroom soup
1 cup milk

Mix ingredients and roll into small meat balls. Brown until crisp in bacon fat or butter. In double boiler combine 1 cup of milk and 1 can mushroom soup. Heat but do not boil. Add browned meat balls to boiler and keep warm until serving.

Serves 2.

SÜSS- SAUER KLOPSE
(Sweet and Sour Meatballs)

1 pound ground beef
1/2 cup onion, chopped
1/2 cup green pepper, chopped
1/2 cup milk
3/4 cup cracker or bread crumbs
salt
pepper

Sauce:

1/4 cup vinegar
1/2 cup catsup
3 tablespoons sugar
1½ tablespoons Worchestershire
sauce

Mix first five items, season to taste and form into small meatballs. Place in casserole. Mix sauce ingredients and pour over meatballs. Cover and bake in medium (350°F.) oven for about one hour. Serve in chafing dish.

HASSENPFEFFER
(Peppery Rabbit Stew)

In Europe, "rabbit" dishes are made with hares. Hares are only distantly related to rabbits. In this country we have two types of rabbit-kin, the jackrabbit, which is really a hare, and the cottontail rabbit. We do not eat jackrabbits today because they are thought to be too tough and gamey. We did, however, when our ancestors arrived in Illinois as evidenced by the Sunday menu at the Mansion House Hotel Dining Room in Belleville in 1850 which offered "Jackass Rabbit", the name by which they were originally known because of their large pointed ears.

Today, German-Americans substitute cottontail or commercially-raised rabbits for hare, while the expensive German restaurants like Lüchow's in New York City, or Tadich's Grill in San Francisco, import Arctic hares from Canada for their "hassen" dishes.

2 cups water
1/2 cup vinegar
3 tablespoons sugar
1 teaspoon salt
1/2 teaspoon whole cloves
1/2 teaspoon whole black pepper
1 bay leaf
1 rabbit, cut up for frying
3 tablespoons butter
1 medium onion
1½ tablespoons flour
1/2 cup sour cream

Mix together first seven ingredients and heat to boiling. Let cool, and place rabbit in glass or enameled bowl and cover with cooled water, vinegar and spice mixture. Cover bowl and refrigerate overnight.

Remove rabbit and brown in hot butter. Strain liquid which rabbit was marinated in pour 1/2 cup of it over rabbit. Cover and simmer one hour or until tender. Add onion and 1/2 cup more of the liquid and continue to simmer until rabbit is extremely tender. Make a paste of flour and water and stir in the liquid the rabbit is cooking in. After about two minutes, stir in sour cream, blend thoroughly, allow to come to a boil and serve at once.

GRATINIERTE SCHWEINEKOTELETTEN
(Pork Chops Au Gratin)

2 3/4 pound pork chops, 1" thick
Potatoes au Gratin (see "Vegetable
and Casserole" chapter)

Prepare Potatoes au Gratin dish and set aside before baking.
Brown pork chops in butter about ten minutes each side and
place on top of potato dish. Bake in medium (350°F.) oven for
about thirty five minutes or until cheese is melted and golden
brown and pork chops are done through. Serves 2

HINT: For an easy alternative to the above. Prepare "Potatoes
Au Gratin" from prepared box mix containing dehydrated
potatoes and cheese sauce in powder form, following
instructions on the box. Brown the pork chops each side in
butter and just when ready to cook the potatoes, place the pork
chops on top of the potatoes in the casserole and bake together.

WESTPHALISCHER SCHENKEN
(Glazed Ham Loaves)

1/2 pound ground cured ham
1/2 pound ground pork
1/3 cup cracker crumbs
1 small onion chopped fine or grated
1 egg, beaten
3/ 4 cup milk
1/4 teaspoon salt
pepper

<u>Syrup</u>:

1 cup brown sugar
3 tablespoons vinegar
1 teaspoon dry mustard

Mix first **8** ingredients together thoroughly and pack into large-sized greased muffin tins. Shape meat so it rounds up well, but does not come to top of pan around the edges. Bake for twenty minutes at 350°F.

Meanwhile, make a syrup by blending sugar, vinegar and dry mustard. Boil together for one minute. When meat loaves have baked for twenty minutes, remove from oven and pour syrup over them. Return to oven for twenty minutes more. Yields 12 small loaves.

GEHACKTES FLEISCH
(Easy Hash)

1 tablespoon shortening
1 medium onion, chopped
1 pound ground round
1 teaspoon salt
2 medium potatoes
1/2 cup steak sauce
1 can Cream of Mushroom soup

Sautè chopped onion in butter until soft, add ground round and brown. Add salt and potatoes which have been peeled and diced. Add steak sauce and mushroom soup mix. Cover and cook over low (325°F.) heat for about 30 minutes, adding water if required, until potatoes are done and mixture has cooked down.

ESCHWEGER KARTOFFELGULASCH
(Eschwege's own Potato Stew)

The Werra Valley Tourist Board contributed this as the favorite dish of their region and, judging from the contributions of others, whether known as Hungarian Goulash, Gulasch Suppe, or Beef Goulash, this is a favorite of a great many German-Americans as well.

1 pound beef chuck, cubed
3 potatoes
2 green peppers
1/2 teaspoon garlic salt
4 cups water
2 or 3 onions
2 cans tomatoes or 3 large tomatoes,
sliced
4 tablespoons cooking oil or butter
2 tablespoons paprika
1 teaspoon caraway seeds
1/2 teaspoon marjoram
salt and pepper
1/2 cup red wine
1/2 cup sour cream

Slice onions very small and sauté in hot oil or butter until transparent. Add meat cubes and brown, stirring often. Add seasonings, potatoes and other ingredients except tomatoes. Add water and let stew for about one hour. When juice has nearly evaporated, add tomatoes, sprinkle with flour and cook together briefly. Add red wine and sour cream just before serving. Serves 2 or 3.

SAUERBRATEN
(Roast Beef)

3-4 pound beef chuck roast
1/2 teaspoon pepper
1/2 teaspoon nutmeg
2 teaspoons salt
1 medium onion, sliced
1 bay leaf
2 tablespoons parsley, chopped
3/4 cup dry white wine or vinegar
3/4 cup water
1/4 cup sugar
2 tablespoons butter
2 tablespoons flour
1/4 cup cream
1/2 cup seedless raisins (optional)

Rub meat with pepper, nutmeg and salt. Place in crock or enamel pan. Add onion, bay leaf, and parsley. Heat water, wine, and sugar to boiling and pour over roast. Cool, then cover and place in refrigerator overnight. (Never soak nor cook sauerbraten in an iron pan).

Drain meat, brown slowly in butter in a heavy skillet, then add 1/2 cup of the liquid in which it was soaked and an onion. Cover and simmer slowly for about three hours, or until the meat is tender, adding more of the liquid as it evaporates. Blend flour and cream and add to strained liquid from meat. Add raisins and stir over direct heat until thick. Serve over meat. Serves 5 to 7.

HINT: Many cooks like to "lard" a lean roast by inserting strips of salt pork or bacon in slashes made in the roast. In cooking, this inserted fat melts and bastes the meat resulting in a more tender and flavorful roast.

ROULADEN
(Beef Roll)

1¾ pound beef steak (round or
sirloin)
1 pound bacon
1 onion
2 mushrooms
¼ cup flour
salt
pepper

Cut thin-sliced beef steaks into four inch square pieces. Place a two inch strip of bacon, a thin slice of onion and diced mushrooms on each steak. Roll them up, tying each with a string or secure with a toothpick. Salt and pepper to taste, coat with flour and brown in oil or butter. Add water and simmer until tender. Add more water from time to time as necessary. Serve the beef rolls covered with their own gravy.

HINT: Some include parsley or even a dill pickle wedge in these beef rolls. One might experiment with cheese or other ingredients.

CASSEROLES and VEGETABLES

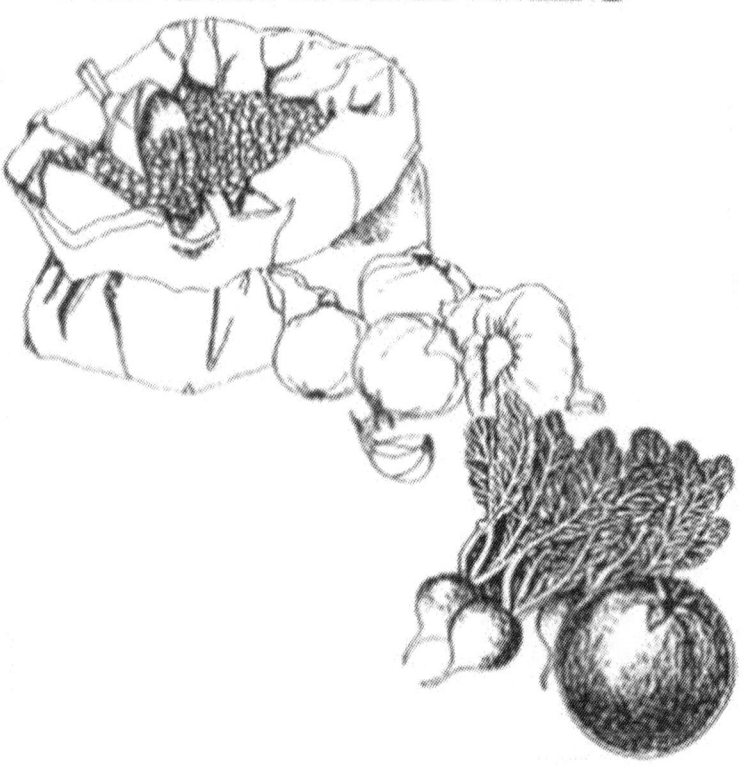

GRATINIERTE KARTOFFELN
(Potatoes *Au Gratin*)

4 large potatoes, thinly sliced
salt
pepper
3 tablespoons butter
1 cup sharp cheddar cheese, grated
1 cup milk

Potatoes must be washed, peeled and carefully dried. Cook potatoes, covered, in butter for six to eight minutes or until tender, stirring occasionally. Place in buttered baking dish. Add milk, season with salt, pepper, and sprinkle with melted butter. Add cheese.

Bake, uncovered, in a medium (350°F.) oven for 35 to 40 minutes or until potatoes are tender, the sauce is bubbly and cheese is melted.

ALLERLEI DEUTSCHES
(German Creamed Vegetables)

The German name for this dish means literally, "a little of everything German". It is representative of the way in which German people prefer their vegetables served in a thickened gravy. Other vegetables may be substituted in this recipe.

1/2 pound asparagus tips
1 cup carrots, cut in 1/2" pieces
1 small cauliflower, divided into
small flowerets
1 turnip, diced
1/3 cup butter
1/4 pound mushrooms, sliced
2 tablespoons flour
salt
pepper

Cook all vegetables but mushrooms in salted water to cover. Drain and set aside liquid. Sauté vegetables together in hot butter for two to three minutes. Remove and keep hot. Sauté mushrooms in same butter, remove, and add to other vegetables. Measure about two cups of the vegetable liquid, stir in flour, and cook over low heat about five minutes, or until it becomes thickened and smooth. Season with salt and pepper. Arrange vegetables on a warm platter, keeping cauliflowerets on top. Pour sauce over the vegetables and serve with any meat dish.

SPINAT NACH DEUTSCHEN ART
(German Style Spinach)

10 oz. fresh spinach
1 cup water
1/2 teaspoon salt
4 slices bacon
2 or 3 tablespoons chopped onion
1½ tablespoons flour
2 teaspoons vinegar (optional)

Wash spinach in cold water. Drain and cut crosswise into 1/2 inch strips. Bring water to boiling in a 3 qt. saucepan. Add spinach, salt and boil for about six minutes or until spinach is tender. Do not drain. Cut bacon into small pieces and sauté in frying pan until brown and crisp. Set bacon aside. In same pan, sauté onions until yellow, add flour and blend well. Drain liquid from spinach and add to onion-flour and bacon drippings; stir until well blended and smooth, then turn into spinach. Continue cooking together with constant stirring until liquid is smooth and thickened. Add pepper, vinegar (optional), place on serving dish and sprinkle the bacon pieces on top.

KARTOFFELKROKETTEN
(Potato Croquettes)

I'll bet you did not know that our ancestors had "Tater Tots". They just called them by another name!

4 large or 5 medium-sized potatoes
salt
pepper
3 tablespoons butter, melted
2 eggs
nutmeg
flour
1 cup bread crumbs
1/4 cup bacon or ham fat

Boil potatoes, peel, and mash free of all lumps. Add melted butter, one whole egg and one egg yolk to the potatoes. Season, blend thoroughly, and allow to cool. Shape into coquettes (since the mealiness of potatoes varies, you may need to add a little flour to hold them together, but not enough to make them "heavy").

Beat remaining egg white, dip croquettes in it, then dip in bread crumbs. Chill thoroughly before frying in deep hot fat (390°F. on a frying themometer) or sufficiently hot that a bread cube dropped into fat will brown in one minute. Drain croquettes on an absorbent paper towel and serve hot. Serves 4.

BOHNENEINTOPF
(Navy Bean Casserole)

1 pound dried navy beans
salt
1 bay leaf
4 medium tomatoes, sliced
4 strips bacon
1 onion, sliced
1/2 cup cheese, grated

Soak dried beans overnight. Cook in salted water with bay leaf for one or two hours or until beans are soft. Arrange alternating layers of beans, sliced tomatoes, lightly fried bacon, and sliced onion in a buttered casserole dish. Top with grated cheese and several dollops of butter and bake in a hot (400°F.) oven for about twenty minutes or until nicely browned. Serves 4.

HINT: Same recipe made with dried peas works as well.

LAUCHGEMÜSE
(Leeks)

In Europe, leeks are so common they are considered "peasant food", while in this country, for some reason, this vegetable is hardly known at all and when the markets do have it, they are expensive and thought of as a gourmet food. Leeks can be served in any way asparagus or celery is prepared but do not overcook, they fall apart easily.

6 leeks
salt
2 tablespoons butter
2 tablespoons flour
1/2 cup milk
water
salt
pepper
nutmeg
2 tablespoons cream

Wash thoroughly and remove green part of leeks from stalks. Cut the rest (white part) in finger-thick slices and grate. Cook ten minutes in boiling salted water, drain, and reserve the water. Prepare a light sauce from butter, flour and milk. Thin with the vegetable water to the desired consistency and season. Add leeks to the sauce and heat through. Add cream, nutmeg, and serve hot. Serves 4.

GEMÜSE MARNAY
(Leeks in Marnay Sauce)

Leeks are excellent served with any rich cheese sauce such as
Marnay Sauce.

Prepare leeks as in above recipe. Boil about ten minutes or until
tender. Place in a casserole, cover with Marnay Sauce (see
chapter on "Sauces"), bake in a hot (400°F.) oven just until all
ingredients are combined. Sprinkle a little extra cheese on top
and serve.

SAUERKRAUT
(Fermented Shredded Cabbage)

1 small onion
2 slices bacon
1 quart sauerkraut
4 beef bouillon cubes
1½ cups water
1 teaspoon sugar
2 tablespoons potato, grated

Cut bacon strips in half and sauté in butter until it begins to
brown, add sliced onion and cook until onion turns transparent.
Add sauerkraut. Dissolve bouillon cubes and sugar in water, add
to kraut mixture. Gently simmer for one hour. Stir in grated
potato and cook an additional 1/2 hour. Serves 4.

HINT: Various recipes call for 1 sliced apple, 1/2 cup white wine,
or cream to be added to the above recipe in lieu of sugar. Also,
1/2 cup of domestic champagne is suggested to be substituted
when served with venison or other wild game.

ROTKOHL MIT APFELN
(Red Cabbage with Apples)

1 medium-size red cabbage
3 tablespoons butter
1 small onion, chopped
1/2 teaspoon salt
2 tart apples, peeled, quartered and
cored
1 tablespoon sugar
1/3 cup vinegar
1/2 teaspoon caraway seed

Quarter cabbage and remove core. Slice coarsely. Sauté onion in butter for about two minutes, add cabbage, apples and salt. Cover with boiling water and simmer in covered skillet for about forty five minutes or until water has almost all evaporated. Stir in sugar and vinegar. Add caraway seed if desired.

ROTKOHL MIT WURST
(Red Cabbage with Sausage)

1 pound sausage links (Knackwurst)
1 tablespoon onions, chopped
2 tablespoons flour
1¼ cup milk
one small head red cabbage
1/2 cup water
1/4 cup sugar
2 teaspoons vinegar
1 teaspoon caraway seed

Sauté sausage and onions in butter over low heat for about 20 minutes. Pour off fat, blend in flour and gradually add milk and salt to taste. Shred cabbage and add to skillet, combine water and sugar and add along with vinegar and caraway seeds. Cover and simmer 20 to 30 minutes, or until tender. Serve with a barbecue sauce. Serves 4.

WESTFÄLISCHER KOHL
(Westphalian Cabbage)

1 cabbage, approx. 2 pounds
3 tablespoons vegetable oil
1 teaspoon salt
1 teaspoon caraway seeds
1 cup beef bouillon
2 or 3 small tart apples
1 tablespoon cornstarch
2 tablespoons cold water
3 tablespoons red wine vinegar
1/4 teaspoon sugar

Shred cabbage. Heat vegetable oil in Dutch oven, add cabbage and sauté for five minutes. Season with salt and caraway seeds. Pour in beef broth, cover and simmer over low heat for about fifteen minutes.

Meanwhile, peel, quarter, core and cut apples into thin wedges. Add to cabbage and simmer another thirty minutes. Blend cornstarch with cold water, add to cabbage and stir until thickened and bubbly. Season with vinegar and sugar just before serving. Serves 4-6.

SCHNITZRÜBEN
(Shredded Beets)

4 cups beets, grated
2 tablespoons butter
4 tablespoons lemon juice
1½ teaspoons
1/2 cup water
2 tablespoons sugar
1/4 teaspoon onion, grated
salt
pepper

Wash beets, peel and grate. Melt butter, add beets, lemon juice, salt and pepper. Check occasionally to see that it does not burn. Add water, sugar, and onion; cover and cook an additional 15 minutes or until beets are tender. Sprinkle with chopped parsley or mint, if desired, and serve.

GETREIDEPUDDING
(Corn Pudding)

This is a German-American recipe using sweet corn (Mais) our ancestors found in abundance in the U.S. Midwest. Getreidepudding means literally "grain pudding".

1 egg, beaten
1 #2 can cream style corn
1 cup milk
1/2 teaspoon salt
1 cup coarse bread crumbs
1/4 cup cheddar cheese, grated

Heat corn and milk and gradually stir in beaten egg. Add salt, bread crumbs and cheese and pour into greased baking dish. Bake uncovered at 350°F. for about thirty minutes or until custard is done.

DEUTSCHE ROTERÜBEN
(German Red Beets)

6 beets
1 tablespoon butter
1 tablespoon flour
2 teaspoons onion, minced
1 cup water
1 tablespoon sugar
2 tablespoons vinegar
1/4 teaspoon salt

Boil beets until tender. Sauté onion in melted butter until yellow. Blend in flour, add hot water and heat until smooth and thickened. Add seasoning and beets. Heat thoroughly.

BOHNEN MIT ÄPFELN
(Beans with Apples)

1 pound dried navy beans
6 cups water
1 teaspoon salt
4 medium-sized tart apples, pared
and sliced
1/3 cup brown sugar
3 slices bacon or salt pork

Wash dried beans and soak overnight. Cook in salted water for between one and two hours or until beans are soft. Drain and save liquid. In a greased baking dish, arrange layers of cooked beans and apples with sugar sprinkled over each layer. Pour in two cups of bean liquid, place bacon or pork slices on top, cover and bake about 2½ hours at 250°F. or until light brown and thoroughly cooked. If ingredients become dry in cooking, add more bean liquid or hot water.

BOHNENKERNE
(Baked Beans)

3 cups canned pork and beans
(2-12 oz. cans)
3 tablespoons brown sugar
1½ tablespoons sorgum molasses
3 slices bacon or salt pork

Mix sugar and sorgum with beans (including liquid in canned beans) and pour in a greased baking dish. Place strips of bacon on top. Bake in slow (300° to 325°F.) oven until thick and brown on top. Cooking time will vary with amount of liquid in canned beans, but allow about four hours. Some recipes reduce this time by using a hotter oven, but great care must be taken as sugar and molasses burn easily at higher temperatures.

RAHMKARTOFFELN
(Creamed Potatoes)

6 potatoes
2 tablespoons butter
3 tablespoons flour
1 cup cream
1 tablespoon parsley, chopped
nutmeg
salt
pepper

Boil potatoes until tender, peel and slice fairly thick. Melt butter, add flour, cream, parsley and seasoning. Heat potatoes thoroughly in this sauce. Serves 4.

HINT: Grated cheddar cheese is often substituted for parsley in this recipe.

BELGRADER SPINAT
(Serbian Spinach)

2 packages frozen spinach
1 pint cottage cheese
6 eggs
1/3 cube butter
1/2 pound cheddar cheese, grated
6 teaspoons flour
salt
pepper

Place all ingredients except spinach in blender. Process until smooth. Combine with spinach. Bake in 350°F. oven for forty minutes. Serves 8.

SPARGELGERICHT
(Asparagus Casserole)

3 eggs, hard-boiled
1½ tablespoons butter
1½ tablespoons flour
3/4 cup milk
1 14½ oz. can asparagus spears, cut
3/4 teaspoon salt
1/2 cup bread crumbs, buttered

Hard-boil eggs, cool and slice. Open can, drain asparagus and save 3/4 cup of the liquid. Make white sauce by melting butter, blend in flour and slowly add milk and asparagus liquid. Stir constantly and cook until smooth.

Fold asparagus into white sauce. In a greased baking dish, arrange a layer of asparagus mixture and then a layer of sliced eggs. Continue to make alternate layers until all ingredients are used.

Melt butter and stir in 1/2 cup bread crumbs until they are coated with butter. Cover with buttered bread crumbs and bake about twenty minutes at 400°F. Serves 4.

RAHMSPARGELN
(Creamed Asparagus)

3/4 pound fresh asparagus
9 almonds, blanched and sliced
3 tablespoons butter
2 tablespoons flour
1/2 cup milk
1/2 cup mushrooms, sliced
1 teaspoon cooking sherry
4 slices toast

Boil asparagus until tender, keep hot and retain liquid. Sauté almonds in butter over medium heat until they just begin to brown. Stir in flour and add milk gradually. Cook, stirring until sauce boils and thickens. Carefully fold in asparagus, 1 cup water that asparagus was cooked in, mushrooms and sherry. Cover and simmer ten minutes. Serve on toast.

HINT: Canned asparagus tips may be substituted and some prefer a white wine to sherry.

SPAGHETTIBRATEN
(Baked Spaghetti)

Although this will not replace the traditional Italian method of preparation of this pasta in my kitchen, I was intrigued by this German spaghetti recipe and found it quite good done this way.

1 pound spaghetti
1 15 ounce can tomato sauce
(1¾ cup)
1 cup water
2 16-ounce cans whole tomatoes
(2 pound)
1 teaspoon red pepper
1/2 teaspoon paprika
1 large onion
4 strips bacon
2 cups sugar

Add 6 teaspoons salt to 6 quarts water and bring to rapid boil. Slowly add spaghetti and let boil for fifteen minutes. Mix together tomato sauce, water, tomatoes which have been broken into small chunks, red pepper, paprika, chopped onion, bacon which has been cut into small pieces, and sugar. Drain cooked spaghetti and combine with tomato mixture, mix well.

Bake covered three hours at 325°F. (or longer at a little lower temperature). Remove cover during the last half hour to assure ingredients have browned and thickened on top.

FRÜHSTÜCKSGERICHT
(Breakfast Casserole)

5 slices white bread
2 cups Cheddar cheese, shredded
2 cups Monterey Jack cheese,
shredded
1 pound Bratwurst, sliced
1/4 teaspoon garlic powder
6 eggs
2 cups milk
1½ teaspoon paprika
1 teaspoon oregano
1/4 teaspoon dry mustard

Trim crust from bread. Cut bread into cubes and place in buttered two-quart (7½ X 11½ inch) baking dish. Sprinkle cheddar cheese over bread cubes. Form layer of sliced bratwurst over cheddar and cover with layer of Monterey Jack cheese.

In separate bowl, beat eggs. Add milk and seasonings. Mix and pour over layered ingredience in casserole. Chill in refrigerator overnight. Bake at 325°F. for one hour. Let stand for fifteen minutes before cutting. Serves eight generously.

HINT: In this recipe, the second cheese may be American or other and Knackwurst, Thüringer, or even cooked pork sausage may be substituted for Bratwurst.

SCHWEINEFLEISCH MIT NUDELN

(Pork and Noodle Casserole)

1/4 pound egg noodles
1½ quarts boiling water
1½ teaspoons salt
3/4 pound ground pork
2 small onions, chopped
2 cups celery, chopped
1 pint fresh mushrooms, chopped
1 can tomato soup
1/3 cup water
3/4 cup cheddar cheese, grated
1 teaspoon salt
1/16 teaspoon pepper

Cook noodles in boiling salted water for about 15 minutes or until tender. Brown meat and add onions, celery, and mushrooms. Cook until vegetables are done. Mix with cooked noodles. Add soup, water, cheese, and season to taste. Place in greased casserole and bake 45 minutes at 350°F.

SALADS

KARTOFFELSALAT
(Potato Salad)

2 pounds potatoes (8 medium-sized)
4 slices bacon, diced
1/4 cup onion, chopped
1 tablespoon flour
2 teaspoons salt
1¼ tablespoons sugar
1/4 teaspoon pepper
2/3 cup cider vinegar
1/3 cup water
1/2 teaspoon celery seed
3 tablespoons parsley, chopped

Boil potatoes in jackets until tender. Let cool, peel and slice thinly. Fry bacon until crisp, add onion and cook one minute more. Blend in flour, salt, sugar, and pepper. Stir in vinegar and water and cook, stirring, ten more minutes. Pour over sliced potatoes, add celery seed and parsley. Serve at once. Serves 4.

KARTOFFELSALAT mit KNACKWURST
(Hot Potato Salad with Knackwurst)

3 cups (5 medium) potatoes, diced
4 strips bacon
1/2 pound (4) knackwurst or
frankfurters, sliced
1/2 cup onion, sliced
1 can (10½ oz.) cream of celery
soup
1/4 cup water (or milk)
2 tablespoons vinegar
2 tablespoons sweet relish

Prepare and boil potatoes until tender. Fry bacon in deep skillet over low heat until crisp, remove, drain and crumble. Sautè wurst slices and onion in bacon drippings until onion is tender. Add soup, water, vinegar, and relish; mix well. Add potatoes, toss lightly and heat. When thoroughly heated, serve hot with crumbled bacon sprinkled on top. Serves 4-6.

GRÜNE-BOHNEN-SALAT (HEISS)
(Hot Green Bean Salad)

1 quart fresh green (string) beans
(1 pound)
1/2 cup onions, chopped
4 tablespoons bacon fat
4 tablespoons vinegar
3 tablespoons sugar
1 teaspoon salt

Wash and cut beans. Cook in salted water about fifteen minutes or until tender, but not soft. Drain, cut into thin strips. Cook onion in hot fat over low heat for about five minutes or until soft. Add beans and other ingredients, mix well and heat through. Serve warm.

GRÜNE-BOHNEN-SALAT (KALT)
(Cold Green Bean Salad)

1½ pounds green beans
1/2 cup pickled sour onions
1/4 cup liquid from sour onions
2 tablespoons salad oil
1/2 teaspoon salt
1/8 teaspoon paprika

Wash beans, cook in boiling water until tender. Drain, cool and cut into thin strips. Combine all ingredients and refrigerate for three hours. Serve on top of lettuce leaves, garnish with pimiento. Serve with mayonnaise or French dressing. Serves 3-4.

SCHWEINEFLEISCH-APFELSALAT
(Pork and Apple Salad)

2 cups cooked pork or ham, diced
2 cups unpared red apples, diced
1 cup celery, diced
1/4 cup sweet relish
1 tablespoon lemon juice
1/4 teaspoon onion juice
salt
1/3 cup mayonnaise (or salad
dressing)

Combine ingredients; chill. Serve on lettuce leaves. Serves 4.

DREIBOHNENSALAT
(Three Bean Salad)

OK, so the recipe calls for four. I don't know why, but this favorite Deli choice is usually called "Three Bean Salad". I will count next time I visit my German Deli counter. I refuse to call it "Vierbohnensalat" so pick any three.

3/4 cup sugar
1/3 cup salad oil
1 teaspoon salt
2/3 cup terragon vinegar
1 #1 can green beans, cut
1 #1 can wax beans
1 #1 can kidney beans, rinsed
1 8 oz. can green lima beans
1 onion, sliced

Combine all of the ingredients. Chill overnight.

KOHLSALAT MIT NÜSSEN UND ÄPFELN
(Cabbage Salad with Nuts and Apples)

1 apple pared, cored and cut up
1 cup sweet crisp cabbage, shredded
1/2 cup black walnuts

Mix ingredients together with 2 tablespoons of mayonnaise or mix a special dressing composed of 1/3 mayonnaise, 1/3 French salad dressing, and 1/3 whipped cream.

TASCHENKREBSSALAT
(Crab Meat Salad)

2 avocados
2 cups canned crab meat, flaked
1 cup celery, diced
1/2 cup mayonnaise
1 tablespoon French dressing
1 teaspoon lemon juice
4 crisp lettuce leaves
salt
pepper

Combine crab-meat and celery. Mix together mayonnaise, French dressing, and lemon juice and add to crab-meat and celery. Season to taste. Peel avocados, cut in half and remove seeds. Place one half an avocado on each lettuce leaf, fill with crab-meat salad and top with a dollop of mayonnaise. Serves 4.

KOHL MIT ANANAS
(Cabbage-Pineapple Slaw)

3 cups cabbage, shredded
1 cup pineapple, crushed
3/4 cup marshmallows, miniature
1/2 cup mayonnaise
1/2 teaspoon salt

Cabbage should be crisp and crushed pineapple well drained. Mix all ingredients together lightly and serve at once.

SAUERKRAUTSALAT MIT SCHINKEN
(Sauerkraut Salad with Ham)

1 16 oz. can sauerkraut
1/2 pound red grapes
6 oz. cooked ham

dressing:

1/2 cup yogurt
1/4 teaspoon salt
1/4 teaspoon pepper
1 teaspoon honey

Rinse and drain sauerkraut. Chop coarsely. Wash grapes and cut in halves; remove seeds if desired. Cut ham into julienne strips. Gently mix these ingredients.

Blend dressing ingredients and stir into sauerkraut mixture. Marinate for ten minutes. Adjust seasoning before serving, if necessary.

Serves 4.

ROTE-RÜBEN-SALAT
(Red Beet Salad)

1 pound red beets
4 tablespoons vinegar
4 tablespoons water
1/2 teaspoon sugar
2 teaspoons caraway seeds
1 small onion, chopped
1 teaspoon cloves, ground
1 bay leaf
salt
pepper
3-4 tablespoons olive oil

Scrub beets and cook in salted water until tender. Dip in cold water, peel and slice thinly. Mix all other ingredients to prepare a marinade, smoothing it out with oil to taste. Pour marinade over beets and let them soak for several hours before serving. Serves 4.

ALTERWIENER SALAT
(Fruit Salad from Old Vienna)

This is a favorite of German tearooms. I first encountered it in Munich. It is really a dessert, maybe called salad so customers will not feel so guilty about ordering such a sweet concoction between meals.

4 oranges, sliced
1/2 cup sugar
2 tablespoons orange juice
2 tablespoons lemon juice
8 small apples

Apple Stuffing:

jam of your choice
butter

Peel oranges and slice. Arrange layers in a glass serving dish, sugaring each layer. Moisten with orange and lemon juice. Peel apples, core and stuff them with jam. Sprinkle with sugar and dollops of butter. Bake in buttered baking dish in 250N F. oven until soft. Cool and place on top of orange salad. Keep in refrigerator until ready to serve. Serve with thick black coffee. Serves 8.

MAKKARONISALAT
(Macaroni Salad)

3/4 cup elbow macaroni
1/4 pound liverwurst, cubed
1/2 cup sweet pickles, chopped
1/2 cup celery, sliced
1/3 cup mayonnaise
2 tablespoons chili sauce
1/2 teaspoon salt

Cook macaroni in salted water, drain and rinse. Combine with liverwurst, pickles, and celery. Blend in remaining ingredients together and toss with macaroni mixture. May be garnished with tomato wedges, green pepper rings or egg slices. Serves 4.

GEFÜLLTE-RÜBEN-SALAT
(Stuffed Beet Salad)

2 or more
cans whole beets, drained
1 part sweet relish
2 parts sour cream
salt

Scoop out center of each beet with a melon ball cutter. Fill beets with a mixture of sweet relish and sour cream, seasoned to taste. Serve three or four stuffed beets on crisp greens with French Dressing. May be garnished with parsley or watercress.

KRAUTSALAT
(Cole Slaw)

1/3 cup mayonnaise
1/2 teaspoon salt
1 dash pepper
1 tablespoon minced onion
4 teaspoons vinegar
1 teaspoon sugar
1 quart shredded cabbage

Combine all ingredients except cabbage in mixing bowl. Add cabbage and mix well. Garnish with parsely.
Serves 6.

KRAUTSALAT NACH WERRATAL ART
(Cole Slaw, The Werra Valley Way)

1 head white cabbage
2 qts. boiling water
2 onions, shredded finely
1 or 2 green peppers, shredded
1/4 cup vinegar
2 egg yolks, beaten
1 teaspoon salt
1/2 teaspoon pepper
3 tablespoons olive oil
1 cup sour cream

Wash cabbage, slice or cut finely. Bring water to boil, add cabbage and boil for five minutes. Drain through colander and press out all water. Mix with onions, green peppers and vinegar. Beat eggs, salt and pepper together, add oil gradually while beating steadily. Pour over cabbage mixture; stir well. Pour sour cream over, stirring until it is well and evenly mixed. Serves 4 or 6.

BAKED GOODS and DESSERTS

PFANNEKUCHEN
(German Pancakes)

In Germany, pancakes are a dessert, not a breakfast food, and are often served covered with powdered cinnamon, sugar, lingonberries or huckleberries, slices of cooked apples or even sometimes a chocolate sauce. They are often served rolled up like a jelly roll. Waiters even do the *flambée* presentation by pouring rum or Kirschwasser on them and igniting it at the table to treat you to the fiery spectacle of bluish flames dancing across your pancake. You won't find that at International House of Pancakes or the Waffle House!

1 cup flour
1 cup milk
2 tablespoons sugar
4 eggs
1 dash nutmeg
1/4 teaspoon cooking oil

Measure flour in large bowl. In smaller bowl, combine all remaining ingredients, beating well. Slowly add egg mixture to flour bowl, beating with a whisk until well blended. Set aside. Heat griddle or teflon-coated skillet to medium high. Brush skillet with cooking oil. Using ladle, scoop approx. 1/2 cup of batter onto hot skillet. Cook until set and bubbly, turn over for ten to fifteen seconds. Serve hot with butter and lemon or blueberry syrup. Yields 6 large pancakes.

KUCHEN
(Coffee Cake)

3 packages yeast
2 tablespoons sugar
1 cup water
1 cup evaporated milk
9 cups flour
1/2 cup butter
1 cup sugar
1/2 teaspoon salt
4 eggs, beaten

Dissolve yeast and sugar in lukewarm water. Add milk and 3 cups of the flour. Beat until smooth, cover and allow about 3/4 hour for it to rise. Cream butter, salt and sugar together and add to yeast mixture. Add well-beaten egg and remaining flour.

Knead until smooth and place in a well-greased bowl. Cover and let rise in a warm place for about two hours or until light. Divide into four portions, roll 1/2 inch thick and place in greased pans (8" X 12" X 2"). Let rise again until light, about another 1½ hours.

Prick tops, brush with melted butter and sprinkle with topping (see below). Let rise about 1/2 hour and then bake at 400°F. about twenty minutes or until done.

STREUSELKUCHEN
(Streusel Topping for Coffee Cake)

2/3 cup butter
2/3 cup sugar
1 cup sifted flour
2 cups dry cake or bread crumbs
2 teaspoons cinnamon

Cream together butter and sugar. Mix in other ingredients.

NUSSKUCHEN
(Honey Nut Topping for Coffee Cake)

1/2 cup butter
1/2 cup sugar
1/2 cup sifted flour
1/2 cup honey
1 cup chopped nuts

Cream together butter and sugar. Add flour and honey, beat until well mixed. Add nuts.

ZIMTKUCHEN
(Cinnamon Topping for Coffee Cake)

3/4 cup butter
1½ cup sugar
3/4 cup sifted flour
3 teaspoons cinnamon
1/4 teaspoon salt

Cream together butter and sugar. Add remaining ingredients and mix well until crumbly.

ORANGENBROT
(Orange Bread)

Rind from 4 oranges, grated
3 teaspoons baking powder
2 cups sugar
2 eggs
1 cup chopped walnuts or pecans
3¼ cups flour
3/4 cup water
2 tablespoons butter
1/2 teaspoon salt
1 cup milk

Mix grated orange rind with water and 1 cup of sugar. Cook until this mixture is about the consistency of applesauce. Set it aside. Blend together the other cup of sugar, eggs (well beaten), milk, flour, baking powder, butter, salt and nuts. When thoroughly mixed, combine with orange peel mixture. Blend well, but do not beat. Pour into two buttered loaf pans and bake at 325°F. for 35 to 40 minutes.

PFLAUMENKUCHEN
(German Plum Cake)

The Germans are extremely fond of open fruit tarts which take the place of our fruit pies. All sorts of fruits are used in making these festive cakes such as apples, pears, gooseberries, peaches, apricots, cherries, and plums. The latter two are particular favorites but any may be substituted for the plums in this recipe although amount of sugar must be adjusted depending on the tartness of the fruit selected.

1 cup flour
2 teaspoons baking powder
1/2 teaspoon salt
1 tablespoon sugar
3 tablespoons butter
1/3 cup milk
1-1½ pounds plums, pitted and
halved
2 egg yolks
2/3 cup heavy cream
1/3 cup sugar
1/2 cup blanched chopped almonds
1/4 teaspoon nutmeg

Sift together flour, baking powder, salt, and sugar. With a pastry blender or two knives, cut in butter until the mixture resembles oatmeal. Add milk and mix just long enough to combine the ingredients.

Butter bottom and sides of a 9-inch shallow cake pan and spread dough in bottom and on sides of the pan. Crimp sides with the tines of a fork. Arrange plum halves, skin side down, over dough in circles, overlapping them slightly. Bake in a medium hot (400°F.) oven for ten to fifteen minutes.

Combine egg yolks, heavy cream, sugar, almonds, and nutmeg. Pour mixture over cake and continue baking for ten or fifteen more minutes or until done. The topping should be set and golden brown.

LEBKUCHEN
(Gingerbread)

2 eggs
1/2 cups brown sugar (packed)
1 cup honey
1 cup sorghum molasses
6 cups flour
2 teaspoons cinnamon
3/4 teaspoons nutmeg
3/4 teaspoons cloves
3/4 teaspoons allspice
1 teaspoon baking soda
1 cup chopped, mixed candied
fruit and peels
1 cup slivered blanched almonds

Beat eggs and beat in sugar. Stir in honey and molasses. Sift and measure flour, add cinnamon, nutmeg, allspice and soda and sift together three times. Stir this mixture into first and add fruit and nuts. Mix well. Chill several hours or overnight in refrigerator.

Roll out on floured board until 1/4 inch thick. Cut into rectangles 2 x 3 inches, place on greased cookie sheet and bake eight to ten minutes at 350°F. When cool, brush top with the following glaze:

Combine 1½ cup sifted powdered sugar, 1½ teaspoon white corn syrup, and add hot water, a teaspoon at a time, until reaching spreading consistency.

HINT: Store gingerbread in a covered tin or cookie jar. It lasts a long time if kept in a cool place.

FRUCHTSPRITZGEBÄCK
(Fruit Cookies)

1 cup butter
2/3 cup sugar
3 egg yolks
1 teaspoon vanilla
2½ cups sifted flour
1/2 teaspoon salt
candied cherries or colored
decorating sugar

Cream butter, add sugar and cream together. Beat in egg yolks and vanilla. Sift together flour and salt and stir into creamed mixture. Using a cookie press, press out dough in different shapes onto an ungreased cookie sheet. Decorate centers of cookies with cherries or colored sugar. Bake at 375°F. for ten minutes or until edges are golden. Makes about 5 dozen cookies.

HASELNUSSTORTE
(Filbert Nut Cake)

This rich torte is perhaps the favorite dessert of all Germans. When properly prepared, it contains no flour. German-Americans often substitute walnuts for filberts in this recipe but it is more delicate and more typically European with filberts.

7 eggs, separated
1½ cup sugar
4½ cup filberts, finely grated
7 additional egg whites
1 cup heavy cream

Beat egg yolks and 1½ cup sugar until very thick and lemon-colored. Add 4 cups grated filberts. Beat all 14 egg whites until stiff but not dry. Fold lightly into mixture. Pour into well buttered and floured 10-inch baking pan. Bake in pre-heated moderate (350°F.) oven forty to forty-five minutes or until done. Turn off heat and leave cake in oven with door open ten more minutes. Cool.

Beat heavy cream with remaining 2 tablespoons sugar until stiff. Fold in remaining 1/2 grated nuts. Cut cake in half and spread with filling.

Frosting For Torte:

2½ cups sifted confectioners'sugar
1 tablespoon grated lemon rind
2 teaspoons butter
2 teaspoons warm water
1 stiffly beaten egg white

Combine sugar, lemon rind, butter, and warm water into a smooth paste. (it may be necessary to add more water, a little at a time) Fold into beaten egg white. Frost cake and decorate with additional filbert halves. Chill in refrigerator for three hours before serving.

GERMAN CHRISTMAS COOKIES

Few culinary traditions are more deeply rooted than those of Germany's Christmas cookies. Many families of German heritage all over the world follow an annual schedule for making the sweets that accompany afternoon coffee or tea and are brought out for visitors who drop by during the holiday season. Beginning in early November, Pfeffernüsse, Lebkuchen, and other honey-based cookies that need to ripen are baked and stashed away in tins. Later the marzipan and sugar cookies, most of which can be eaten the same day they are baked, and brightly-painted Springerle, join them on a pleasing holiday plates.

HICKORYNUSSKEKSE
(Hickory Nut Kisses)

Our immigrant family, living as they did surrounded by the hardwood forests of Southern Illinois, enjoyed these simple cookies. I suspect the idea was born in the Hainich forest of Thüringen.

4 egg whites
2 cups sugar
4 cups ground hickory nuts
3/4 teaspoon baking powder
1/2 cup cake flour

Beat egg whites until stiff. Fold in sugar, sifted flour, baking powder and nuts. Drop dollops onto greased cookie sheet and bake about twenty minutes in a 325°F. oven. Remove from pan immediately.

NUSSKUGELN
(Nut Balls)

1 cup butter
1/2 cup powdered sugar
2¼ cup sifted flour
1/4 teaspoon salt
1 teaspoon vanilla
3/4 cup pecans, finely chopped

Cream together butter and sugar. Fold flour and salt into creamed mixture (may be worked in by hand). Add vanilla and nuts. If mixture becomes too sticky, chill dough. Form dough into small balls and bake on greased cookie sheet for fourteen to twenty minutes at 400°F. Watch closely at end of baking time as these brown suddenly! While still warm, roll each ball in powdered sugar.

WEIHNACHTSPFEFFERNÜSSE
(Christmas Peppernuts)

These cookie balls are traditionally baked at Christmastime in German kitchens all over the world.

2 eggs
2 cups brown sugar (packed)
1 tablespoon hot water
2 cups sifted flour
1 teaspoon baking soda
1/4 teaspoon salt
1/2 teaspoon cinnamon
1/4 teaspoon mace
1 cup chopped walnuts
1 pinch white pepper
powdered sugar

Beat eggs until very light. Add sugar, tablespoon at a time, continuing to beat. Dissolve soda in hot water and stir in. Sift flour, salt and spices together and add to mixture. Stir in nuts. Chill dough, shape into small balls, place on lightly greased cookie sheet, bake at 375°F. for six to eight minutes or until lightly browned.

Do not overbake as these cookie balls should be soft in the center. Remove from oven and roll at once in powered sugar.

APFELTORTE
(German Apple Cake)

1 cup butter
1 cup sugar
2 eggs
1¾ cups flour
2 teaspoon baking powder
8-10 cooking apples, peeled and
thinly sliced
Cinnamon

Melt butter, gradually add sugar and beat well. Sift flour and baking powder, beat into creamed mixture. Spread on bottom of greased pan. Stand apples on end in cake batter (it will look like a chrysanthemum of apple slices). Sprinkle with cinnamon and bake in preheated 350°F. oven for an hour.

Topping:

1/2 cup butter
1 cup sugar
2 eggs

Cream butter and sugar. Beat in two eggs. Pour over top of baked torte, return to oven for fifteen minutes at 325°F. Serves 12.

SPRINGERLE
(Sweet German Pastry)

Here is another treat found in many German and German-American homes at Christmastime and on special days.

4 eggs
4 cups confectioners' sugar (1lb.)
10 drops anise oil
4 cups flour, sifted
1 teaspoon baking soda
anise seed (optional)

Beat eggs until very light. Add sugar, teaspoon at a time, continue beating until it appears as as soft meringue. (approx. 15 minutes with mixer at high speed or 1/2 hour by hand).

Add anise oil, blend in sifted flour and soda. Cover and let stand fifteen to twenty minutes. Roll out a small portion at a time on floured board to about 1/4 inch thickness. Cut with cookie cutter or pastry wheel into desired shapes. (traditional German kitchens have Springerle molds which give the dough distinctive impressions). When dough has been cut into cookie-sized portions, cover with a towel and allow to dry overnight at room temperature away from children.

Place on greased cookie sheet and sprinkle with crushed anise seed.

Bake at 300°F. for about twenty minutes or until they are light straw-colored.

HINT: After baking and cooling, Springerle are traditionally decorated by painting with a paint brush dipped in water-diluted food coloring. They are usually of light pastel colors. Store in air-tight tin or cookie jar.

RHABARBERTORTE
(Rhubarb Torte)

Crust

1 cup butter
2 cups flour
2 tablespoons sugar

Cut butter into flour and sugar mixture until crumbly. Press into
9 x 13 inch pan. Bake at 350°F. for fifteen minutes.

Filling

6 egg yolks
1 cup sweet cream
1/2 teaspoon salt
2 cups sugar
2 tablespoons flour
5 cups rhubarb, finely cut

Meringue Topping

6 egg whites, beaten
1 teaspoon vanilla
12 tablespoons sugar
1/4 teaspoons salt

Mix up meringue topping and spread over custard. Return to
oven until lightly browned.

BLITZTORTE
(Quick Cake)

Layers:

1/2 cup butter or shortening
1/2 cup sugar
4 egg yolks
1a cups cake flour, sifted
1a teaspoons baking powder
5 tablespoons milk

Cream butter, add sugar gradually and cream until light and fluffy. Add egg yolks, one at a time, and beat well. Sift flour and baking powder together. Add flour alternately with milk, adding flour in three parts and milk in two. Spread into two nine-inch layer pans which have been greased and floured.

Topping:

4 egg whites
1 cup sugar
1¼ cups almonds, shredded

Beat egg whites until stiff, then add sugar gradually while continuing to beat. Spread equal amounts on top of each cake layer. Sprinkle each with almonds. Bake at 325°F. for twenty-five minutes, then increase to 350°F. and bake for thirty minutes more.

Put the two layers together using whipped cream. Serve with ice cream.

HINT: Some prefer to omit nuts and substitute fruit between the layers. Also, custard may be substituted for whipped cream.

SCHNITZBROT
(Fruit Bread)

Dried fruit is used to give this bread its distinctive flavor. The fruit is cut up (schnitz), hence the name. Some recipes call for anise seeds.

1 12-ounce package mixed dried fruit
1 8-ounce package dried apples
1 package or cake of yeast
1/4 cup lukewarm water
1 tablespoon sugar
1½ cups likewarm scalded milk
8½ cups flour, unsifted
1/2 cup butter or shortening
1 cup sugar
2 eggs, well beaten
1 teaspoon salt
1/2 teaspoon cinnamon
3/4 cup raisins
3/4 cup currants
1 cup nuts (optional)

Cover the mixed dried fruit and apples with water and soak overnight. Boil about fifteen minutes or until fruit is quite soft. Drain in a colander and cut up the fruit.

Soften yeast in warm water, add 1 tablespoon sugar and let stand ten minutes. Add milk and 1½ cups of flour. Set aside until bubbles break on top.

Cream butter, add 1 cup sugar and mix in beaten eggs. Add the yeast mixture, chopped fruit, salt, cinnamon, raisins, currants and nuts. Beat in three cups of flour.

Take out 1/4 of the dough and knead on a floured pastry cloth, adding enough flour to keep dough soft, but not sticky. Continue doing this three more times until all the dough has been worked up. Knead it all together and place it in a greased bowl. Cover and place it in a warm place until it doubles in bulk.

Knead lightly and separate dough into four portions. Place each in a greased bread pan, cover and wait until they double in bulk. Bake at 400°F. for ten minutes, reduce heat to 350°F. and bake forty-five minutes longer or until they are done.

SAUCES and MISCELLANY

SPÄTZLE
(German Pasta)

4 cups flour
3 eggs
1 cup water
1 tablespoon salt

Prepare a firm dough from the flour, eggs, water, and salt. Beat until it comes easily away from the sides of the bowl. Form strips and cook them in boiling saltwater.

Skim them out, dip in cold water, and serve on a hot platter. Some prefer to brown the Spätzle lightly in butter before serving. This is a favorite accompaniment to various meat and vegetable dishes.

KÄSESOSSE
(Mornay Sauce)

This rich cheese sauce can be used to make any egg, fish, vegetable, or white meat dish into something special. Other cheeses may be substituted for the ones specified.

3 tablespoons butter
3 tablespoons flour
1/2 tablespoon salt
1/4 tablespoon pepper
3/4 chicken bouillon
3/4 cup cream
1 small onion, whole
1 clove garlic
1/2 cup Parmesan Cheese, grated
1/2 cup Swiss Cheese, grated

Melt butter and remove from heat. Blend in flour and seasonings. Gradually add hot bouillon and cream, stirring constantly until smooth. Add onion and cook over low heat, stirring until thick and smooth. Continue cooking about five minutes longer. Remove onion and garlic. Add cheese and stir until well blended. Yields 1-1/2 to 2 cups sauce.

SHALLOTTENSOSSE
(Shallot Cream Sauce)

Shallots are mild-flavored onions which grow in clusters. Each bulb has a reddish or purple skin. This is a favorite German vegetable that is readily available in American markets. What makes this recipe special is that the shallots are roasted in the German manner and not sautéd as Americans more commonly treat them. This sauce can make a mundane meat, poultry or vegetable dish exceptionally flavorful without being extremely heavy.

10 shallots
4 garlic cloves
1/4 cup olive oil
6-8 ounces mixed wild mushrooms
(oyster, morel or stemmed
shiitake, if available)
1 teaspoon dried rosemary
3/4 teaspoon dried rubbed sage
1/2 cup dry Marsala
1½ cup dry light sherry
1½ cup chicken stock or canned low
salt chicken broth
1 cup whipping cream
salt and pepper

Preheat oven to 300°F. Combine olive oil, shallots, and garlic cloves in a small glass baking dish. Cover dish with foil and roast for about one hour or until the shallots are pale golden and tender. Cool slightly until temperature allows handling. Squeeze the shallots and garlic cloves out of their skins (this method saves the step of peeling them before roasting).

Thinly slice both. Retain the oil from the dish. Cover the shallots and garlic separately and store overnight in the refrigerator.

Transfer one tablespoon of the oil from the shallot roasting dish to a heavy large saucepan. Heat oil over medium-high heat. Add the mushrooms, rosemary, sage, sliced shallots and garlic cloves to the saucepan. Add the Marsala and sherry and boil for about six minutes or until syrupy. Add chicken stock (or canned broth) and continue to boil for an additional ten minutes or until the liquid is reduced by about one half.

Add one cup whipping cream and continue to boil another five minutes or until mixture thickens to a sauce-like consistency. Season carefully to taste with salt and pepper.

HINT: Although recipe calls for both a Marsala and a light sherry, since Marsala is just one variety of light sherry from Sicily, I see no reason for requiring two types of cooking wine. Also, any fresh mushrooms may be substituted for the wild varieties specified if not available.

MAIWEIN
(May Wine)

This is not just a recipe, it is a custom I ran into in the Hessian Rhineland region of our homeland and was more than a bit surprised to find it had been imported with our ancestors intact and even now practiced in Southern Illinois thousands of miles from any wine-growing region I am aware of. It goes like this: the first day of May in that region of Hessen lying along the Rhine River is celebrated not with the flying of red flags, marching of units of the people's army or even dancing around a may pole. It is the day set aside for celebrating the harvest of Rhineland grapes for the current year. All over the region family groups of a dozen or so get together to make May wine which is Rhine wine to which is added an extract of *Waldmeister*, an herb grown in Germany and here known as woodruff. Symbolically, woodruff is tied in bunches and added to last year's Rhine wine and allowed to steep for several days. This is said to impart a beneficence on it. Then, when ready, this wine is blended with the new Rhine wine, thus enriching it with a flavor said to be truly inimitable. This May wine is served in large, gaily decorated punch bowls in which float succulent wild strawberries. Thus is the custom, accompanied by appropriate music, folk dancing and wine tasting at the various village wine gardens and vineyards along the river. It's a good time.

In Southern Illinois the May Day custom is preserved but scaled back to single family observations and a more modest recipe.

2 quarts white Moselle or Rhine wine
1 ounce or spray of woodruff
1/4 pound sugar
1 quart pineapple juice
1 cup fresh strawberries

Wash herbs, place woodruff in a covered dish, sprinkle with sugar and set aside. After standing for several hours, pour 1/2 bottle of wine over the sugered woodruff, cover, and leave in the refrigerator overnight. When ready to serve, add the rest of the wine and sugar and chill well. Serve from a punch bowl to which has been added ice, pineapple juice and fresh strawberries.

HINT: Some suggest champagne or carbonated water as added enhancements. I would like to think that the May Day celebration is an old Setzekorn tradition, as well, although I was not aware of it until this project. If not, t should be. If your family observes May Day in this way, let me know. It will make my day.

PREISELBEERENSAFT
(Mulled Cranberry Punch)

1 quart cranberry juice cocktail
2 cups apple cider
1/4 cup golden raisins
5 whole cloves
5 whole allspice

Combine cranberry juice, cider, and raisins in medium-size saucepan. Tie cloves and allspice in a cheese- cloth bag and add to pan. Heat slowly about five minutes or until warm. Remove spice bag. Ladle into stemmed glasses, adding some of the raisins to each. Serves 8.

COGNAKKAFFEE
(Cognac Coffee)

6 eggs, chilled
1 lemon peel, grated
1/2 cup sugar
3 cups strong brewed coffee, cold
2/3 brandy or cognac

Beat eggs and lemon peel until light and fluffy. Add sugar gradually and continue to beat until thick. Stir in coffee slowly, then add brandy. Serve in chilled glasses. Makes 12 1/2 cup servings.

INDEX

Notes

Notes

Notes

Notes

Notes

Notes

ABOUT THE AUTHOR

William Setzekorn is a retired architect, writer and author. His major design projects have included hospitals, schools, shopping centers and civic buildings throughout California and the Pacific Northwest. He is well known for his professional contributions to disaster recovery, having served as consultant to government agencies in South Carolina following Hurricane Hugo, Northern California following Loma Prieta Earthquake, and in Los Angeles following the Northridge Earthquake. He provided design and construction management for experimental earthquake and hurricane- resistant housing on the Island of Guam developed jointly by U.S. and the Island Government and served on Governor Keating's twelve-man task force following Oklahoma City bomb disaster of 1995 which prepared the disaster survey report presented to Congress.

He is author of five published books and contributor to over forty national magazines on diverse subjects. He has just completed a screenplay based on the life of Grace O'Malley a 17th century Irish queen. Writing assignments have taken him to Central America, Europe, Near East, Pacific Islands and Asia. In 1986, at the request of the Franciscan friars in Jerusalem, he studied the results of archaeological work at Emmaus, El-Qubeibeh, made measured drawings on site and did an architectural rendering of a Crusader Castle once located at this shrine. This work was published in *Holy Land Magazine*, *Omnibus*, and elsewhere. Besides cooking, his hobbies include travel, heraldry, yachting, and racing Arabian horses on the California county fair circuit.